The Loire Castles

Over the finest stately homes of the past shine sporadic bursts of passing fame and brief moments of human happiness. Yet, victorious in their battle against the onslaught of time, they remain a heritage of incalculable worth.
It is in the Loire valley that this glorious artistic movement, one of the most attractive features of the entire Renaissance, can be seen and admired.

Armel de Wismes

Castles are a reflection of eternity. Often, a castle can be seen rising above a village or town, and it is impossible to remain indifferent to its beauty.
In a country as old as France, the castles are a visible proof of a rich and varied past, and those standing along the banks of the Loire are the most precious remains of the French Renaissance.
The illustrations to this book show the finest of these castles. Some are still fortified; others have been transformed or rebuilt. At the beginning of the XV century, when the whole of the north of France belonged to the English, the country's most characteristic river remained French. It was as if the Loire had formed a barrier against the invader. When peace returned, Touraine, which had been one of the strongest bastions of the monarchy, enjoyed a period of calm. Everywhere, magnificent gothic architecture sprang up and the first winds of the Renaissance began to blow around the walls of the powerful fortresses. A few years later, the last of the Valois built their new palaces in this area alone. From Charles VII to Henry III, the French court became one of the most outstanding in the world. The most famous architects of the day were sponsored by the royal family and by other patrons of the arts.
Amboise, Blois, Chambord, Chenonceau, Montsoreau... Names that hark back to a fascinating period of history: a period of battles and romance, refinement and cruelty, of murky plots and stirring adventures...

ARTAUD FRERES PUBLICATION
Photos ARTAUD Frères and la Goélette
44470 Carquefou - Nantes - Tel. (40) 30-26-56

Printed in the E.E.C.

Text by Armel de Wismes

The Loire Castles

ARTAUD FRERES PUBLICATION

GENEALOGIE DES ROIS DE FRANCE

	ROIS	NAISSANCE	AVENEMENT	MORT	REINES	NAISSANCE	MORT
	Louis IX (Saint Louis)	1214	1226	1270	Marguerite de Provence	1219	1295
Robert de Clermont + Souche des Bourbons	+ Philippe III le Hardi	1245	1270	1285	Isabelle d'Aragon	1247	1271
Louis de Bourbon	+ Philippe IV	1268	1285	1314	Jeanne de Navarre	1273	1305
+ Jacques de Bourbon — Charles de Valois Souche des Valois	+ Louis X	1289	1314	1316	Clémence de Hongrie	1293	1328
+ Jean de Bourbon	+ Philippe V	1293	·1316	1322	Jeanne de Bourgogne	1294	1329
+ Louis de Bourbon	+ Charles IV	1294	1322	1328	Blanche de Bourgogne	1296	1327
+ Jean de Bourbon	Philippe VI	1293	1328	1350	Jeanne de Bourgogne	1293	1348
+ François de Bourbon	+ Jean II	1319	1350	1364	Bonne de Luxembourg	1316	1349
+ Charles de Bourbon	+ Charles V	1338	1364	1380	Jeanne de Bourbon	1338	1378
Louis d'Orléans	+ Charles VI	1368	1380	1422	Isabeau de Bavière	1371	1435
Jean Comte d'Angoulême Souche des Valois-Angoulême — Charles d'Orléans Souche des Valois-Orléans	+ Charles VII	1403	1422	1461	Marie d'Anjou	1404	1463
	+ Louis XI	1423	1461	1483	Charlotte de Savoie	1442	1483
	+ Charles VIII	1470	1483	1498	Anne de Bretagne fut également femme de Louis XII	1477	1514
Charles, Comte d'Angoulême	Louis XII	1462	1498	1515	Jeanne de France	1464	1505
	François 1er	1494	1515	1547	Claude de France	1499	1524
	+ Henri II	1519	1547	1559	Catherine de Médicis	1519	1589
	+ François II	1544	1559	1560	Marie Stuart	1542	1587
	* Charles IX	1550	1560	1574	Elisabeth d'Autriche	1555	1592
	* Henri III	1551	1574	1589	Louise de Lorraine	1554	1601
	Henri IV	1553	1589	1610	Marie de Médicis	1573	1642
	+ Louis XIII	1601	1610	1643	Anne d'Autriche	1601	1666
+ Philippe, duc d'Orléans + Souche de la maison d'Orléans	+ Louis XIV	1638	1643	1715	Marie Thérèse d'Autriche	1638	1683
Philippe, Régent sous Louis XV	+ Louis Grand Dauphin						
	+ Louis, Duc de Bourgogne						
	+ Louis XV	1710	1715	1774	Marie Leczinska	1703	1768
Louis (le Savant)	* Louis, Dauphin						
+ Louis-Philippe	+ Louis XVI	1754	1774	1793	Marie Antoinette	1755	1793
	* Louis XVIII	1755	1814	1824	Louise Marie - Joséphine de Savoie	1753	1810
	* Charles X	1757	1824	1835	Marie Thérèse de Savoie	1756	1805
	+ Charles, Duc de Berry	1778		1820			
	+ Henri, Comte de Chambord	1820		1883			
Louis-Philippe-Joseph (Egalité)	Louis-Philippe 1er	1773	1830	1850	Marie-Amélie de Sicile	1782	1866

LEGENDE

Fils : + ou └──

Frere : *

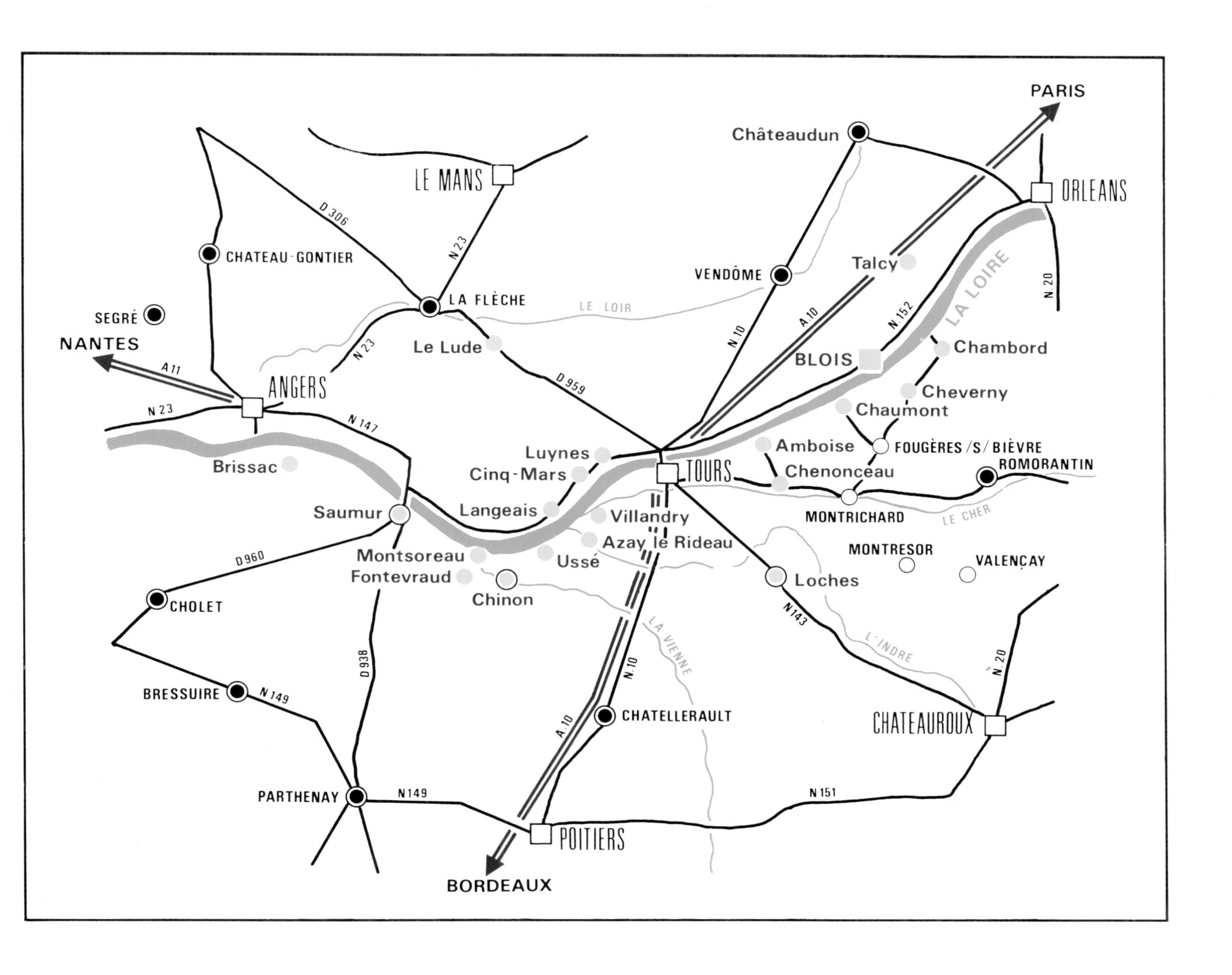

Amboise

A feudal fortress built on the site of a former Roman camp

A visitor to the castle of Amboise will doubtless imagine the kings who lived there, while perhaps forgetting the more distant history of the site... For on the spot where it rises proudly with its massive towers, flamboyant sculpted decorations, there used to be a Gallo-Roman camp, and it was on the Isle d'Or, on the Loire, that Clovis and his enemy, the visigoth Alaric, met to make peace. Later on, Louis le Begue gave Amboise to the Comte d'Anjou. On the rocky promontory, perfectly suited to military skills, a vassal family to the Angevin counts had built a strong fortress. Louis d'Amboise — the last of the landlords from that illustrious lineage, referred to as the race of Mars, was one of Charles VII's most trustworthy captains. However he made the mistake of joining a conspiracy to eliminate Georges de la Tremouille, the king's detested advisor. The plot failed and Louis d'Amboise was condemned to death. All his property was confiscated. He was later pardoned, and he managed to recoup much of his estate. However, Amboise and Chateau Gontier were annexed to the crown in 1434. Charles VII bolstered up the castle ramparts, and built the clock tower; two years later he sent his son the dauphin Louis, aged 13, to Amboise. Louis' marriage had just been celebrated in Tours.

The castle of Louis XI

Charles VII's favourite residences were Chinon and Loches. After a long period of exile, Louis XI took over his father's throne, returning to take up residence in the castle of Amboise with his wife, Queen Charlotte of Savoy. Amboise was an austere home. But this was of little importance. The monarch was a suspicious man, and, in his opinion, the most important thing was to have a good pack of hounds to hunt the deer and wild boar in the neighbouring forest...

In 1469, Louis was obliged to ratify the shameful treaty which his Burgundian cousin had imposed upon him after the stormy meeting at Peronne where Louis had been led into a trap. This debacle was a great humiliation to him. On his return he took two measures which illustrate the extent of his discontent. The eternally rebellious Parisians had trained their parrots to screech "Peronne, Peronne". In order to put an end to this insulting joke, the king had all the parrots seized and brought to Amboise. Then to get revenge on his minister Cardinal Labalue, who had betrayed him, he arrested him and locked him in an iron cage.

In the same year of 1469 the king started a grand order of knights, "a fine and redoubtable order in honour of Monsieur Saint Michel, prince of knighthood in paradise". The 36 dignitaries of this "aymable compagnie" promised mutual assistance to each other and swore an oath of unflinching fidelity to the grand master, in other words, to the king himself. In point of fact, the cautious monarch was only trying to increase his political power when drawing up the statutes of his order.

Under Charles VIII the finest hours of Amboise

The finest hours of Amboise began with the reign of Charles VIII. Under Louis XI, the only occasions for festivity were marriages or receptions given for princes or foreign ambassadors. At these times, the king's followers were expected to be richly clad, but in his day-to-day life, Louis lived very simply with a few intimate friends who shared his tastes and carried out his policies. Charles VIII, a very different man from his father, wanted to make his court one of the most outstanding in the world. At the same time, the court retained the last vestiges of the chivalry of the previous era. His wife Anne, daughter of the last and most festive of the dukes of Brittany, was delighted to participate in the activity. Anne was the first queen to have a train of ladies and maids in waiting who were permanently accomodated in the royal residence. She required strict tidyness within the house, and a spirit of common sense and truthfulness. Charles and Anne dabbled in literature and the arts. They invited poets, painters and sculpters, such as the father of the poet, Jean Marot, Jean Bournichon, illustrator of their hour books, Michel Colombe, the sculptor of Francois de Bretagne's magnificent tomb, in Nantes, considered to be a masterpiece of late medieval sculpture.

Charles VIII's residence soon proved too small to house the artists, courtiers, the French, Scottish and Breton guards, all the government and court services and all the jewellers, tapestry weavers and other master craftsmen. The young king decided to enlarge his castle. He was impatient to see the project finished and called upon the services of the best builders. Raymond de Dezest was in charge of the work. Colin Biart, Guillaume Senault, Louis Armanjart, the master masons, had 170 masons and 90 workmen under their orders. Corneille de Neve and Cassin d'Ultrecht, both Flemish, sculpted the stone lacework in the chapel, and based their work on the fabulous tales of Saint Habert and Saint Christophe. The workmen often laboured by candlelight; in winter they kept warm by heating the stones. Swift progress was made; the King's residence, overlooking the Loire, began to take shape, with its skylights and decorated pinnacles; on the roof terrace side, the delightful outline of the chapel, dedicated to the patron saint of hunting, could be seen. Like his father, Charles was a keen huntsman who even used leopards in his pack. So far, the castle betrayed no Italian influence. The king, an enthusiastic reader of tales of chivalry, soon left Amboise for Lyon, and from there he crossed the Alps to claim the throne of Naples.

During the journey, he was deeply impressed by the lavish Italian palaces. He had soon assimilated the styles of their rich owners, whose personal whims and fancies were always so costly.

He particularly admired the harmonious layout of the gardens. He wrote, "it seems that only Adam and Eve are missing to turn these lands into an earthly paradise". On his return, Dom Pacello was ordered to create a palace garden on the Amboise terrace.

Charles VIII returned with cartloads of objets d'art, paintings, marbles and crystals "weighing 87,000 pounds" to decorate his castle. He brought back architects, carpenters, stonecutters and gardeners. The great merit of Guido Massino, known as Paginino, of Jerome Pacherot, an ornamentalist, of Dominique de Cortone, le Boccador, Fra Giocondo, the engineer, or of Dom Pacello, the master gardener, was to have perfectly integrated the Italian style within a monumental ensemble that remained gothic. This can be seen in the Minime Tower or the vault centres where the lower parts are still medieval, while the sculptures in the upper section discreetly testify to a new art form.

Charles VIII was delighted to have brought these great and talented artists back from the princes and patrons of Italy to use their skills in his court. He paid them generously. His new palace, at the heart of a fortress, mirrored the royal dignity in its magnificence. Commynes says "it was an undertaking characteristic of the young king who never gave a thought to death, rather he hoped for a lengthy life"...

On the 7 February, 1498, Charles came to find the queen to take her to watch a game of "paume" in the castle gardens. He struck his forehead against the lintel of a low door in the Haquelebac gallery, and died that evening of a cerebral haemorrage. Queen Anne was so struck by grief that she shut herself in her room for two days "hoping to follow the path of her husband". The natural goodness of Charles overshadowed the qualities which he may have lacked. He was lamented by the entire kingdom.

Queen Anne dressed in mourning in black, contrary to the custom followed by previous queens who had always worn white.

1

1 - The royal dwelling
2 - The royal castle facade
3 - The castle, the gardens and the Loire

4 - St. Hubet's Chapel (XVth century)
5 - St. Hubert's Chapel spandrel

Louis XII enlarges the castle before abandoning it for Blois

Louis XII, in order to hold on to his Breton heritage, broke off his marriage with the pious Jeanne de France and married the widow of his predecessor. Amboise was stamped with the imprint of Charles VIII; the new king preferred to install his court at Blois. Moreover, he was as keen on saving money as Charles had been on spending it. To reduce taxation, he cut the charges for showing official plays; this was such an unusual initiative that he became known as the "father of the people". However, he never forgot Amboise where his father, the prince and poet Charles of Orleans, had ended his days. He built the long gallery and the balcony on the side of the Minimes convent, while completing the tower named after the latter and the Hurtault tower. After 1499, Louis XII offered Amboise to Louise de Savoie and her two children: Marguerite, aged 8, who was to become the famous Marguerite of Navarre, and Francois d'Angoulème, who inherited the throne.

The glorious era of Francis I

As soon as he took the throne, Francis I confirmed the privilege of the inhabitants of Amboise in memory of the "pleasures and recreations" offered at the castle. The king was particularily interested in architecture; moreover, he was particularly partial to luxury in all its forms, however grandiose and costly. He completed Blois and Amboise and ordered work to begin on Chambord. While this gigantic hunting lodge was being inaugurated, the fleur de lys fluttered on the flags and standards, blown by the Loire winds, on the towers of Amboise. In the castle which, as in the days of Charles VIII, became the centre of political life, balls, feasts and tournaments were the order of the day. Seated on his terrace, the "Grand roi Francois" received the ambassadors of the pope, of the Emperor, and of the dreadful Henry VIII of England in pomp and magnificence. Francis had humiliated Henry VIII with his display of wealth at their meeting on the Field of the Cloth of Gold.
For a long time Amboise was to remember the fabulous revels organised prior to the departure of the knight king for Italy on the occasion of the marriage between Antoine of Lorraine and Renee of Bourbon. As entertainment for the five principal guests, a combat of wild beasts had been carefully prepared. A four-year old boar, just captured from the forest, burst from its cage and rushed up a staircase to burst into the royal stand where Francis was sitting. The chronicler recounts that "the king made all those in his presence withdraw. He was never without a good and trusty sword which he immediately drew from its scabbard. When the boar saw the king draw near, it charged him, thinking it would deal him a deathly wound. But the king advanced half a step, and with his goodly sword, struck him with such force that the weapon went right through its body".

Francis I and Leonardo da Vinci

Francis I was the "father of hunting"... but also "protector of literature and the arts." In January 1516, he persuaded Leonardo da Vinci to take up residence nearby, in the Clos Lucé manor. The monarch welcomed the famous tuscan with all the fitting ceremony. He often visited him and knew him as "my master" or even "my father" and asked him to organise his various festivities. Vinci offered to design him an ingenious system for harnessing the waters of the Loire. This project never came into being. Vinci died on 2nd May, 1519 in the Clos-Lucé and was buried in the Saint Florentin College in the castle. To the monarch who had offered him such warm hospitality and admiration, he left in his will the Mona Lisa and two other works of art, a painting of Saint Anne and another of Saint John the Baptist.

A fascinating meeting with Leonardo, the engineer

You will find within the familiar atmosphere of a dwelling which was lived in and completely furnished with period furniture. Leonardo da Vinci's bed-chamber, his kitchen with its monumental chimney-piece, beautiful Renaissance rooms with bricks and stones splendidly restored by the Beaux-Arts, three lovely XVIIIth century drawing-rooms rich with the grace belonging to Louis XVth's century.
An Italian Renaissance garden, full of roses, in beautiful shady grounds, crossed by a stream, where you can take a rest.

4

5

The discovery of a secret underground passage

A delightful little chapel built by Charles VIIIth for his wife, Anne de Bretagne, along with a secret underground passage which leads to Amboise castle, the mysterious entrance to which can be visited at the Clos-Lucé.

Charles Quint's visit

Amboise, where the dauphin was baptised and Lorenzo de Medici was betrothed to Madeleine of La Tour d'Auvergne, was also the setting for the arrival of the Emperor Charles I of Spain, who had asked for the right of passage through the kingdom of France, on his way to subdue his subjects in the Low Countries. Francis I was not naturally a vengeful man, generally preferring to dazzle his visitors. He decided to receive his former enemy in fine style: as the chronicler tells "so as to make the arrival the more magnificent, the king ordered it to take place at night. He was to arrive at one of the towers, decked out with all imaginable ornaments and garnished with flaming torches giving as much visibility as in the country at noontide. This magnificent reception could have been a disaster... One of the torchbearers had set fire to a tapestry, and the smoke was so dense that the Emperor might have been suffocated...".
At the end of his reign, Francis I left Amboise and Blois, both large palaces designed for sumptuous ceremony. After his death, Henry II and Catherine of Medici entered Amboise beneath a dais of satin damasc and gold thread. Four finely clad ladies welcomed the royal couple with musicians. They chose this castle to bring up their children, and they often came to visit them with all their following. Francois Clouet painted striking portraits of the young princes.

The tumult of amboise

Sixteenth century customs were an astonishing mixture of cortesy and coarseness, of refinement and barbarism. After the reigns of Francis I and Henry II, the country went through the horrors of civil war. The protestants were organised under the military leadership of Conde and Coligny. They fought the catholics under the Duke of Guise. King Francis II had just married Mary Stuart. He was a frail young man, already marked by death. His mother, Catherine of Medici ruled in his name and was supported by the Guise family. Because the Loire valley was considered to be the healthiest region in France, the court moved to Blois.
The protestants amassed their forces in Nantes in 1560 and decided to attack Blois to take as prisoner the Duke and Cardinal of Guise and to leave the king in the hands of the princes. The secret leader of this plot was the Prince of Conde but he confided his organisation to Jean Barri de la Renaudie, known as "La Foret", who was a brave and determined captain who had in his turn recruited a number of partisans and mercenaries. A Parisian lawyer, Pierre des Avenelles, decided, despite the fact that he was a protestant, to reveal the plot which was being hatched to the Duke de Guise. Since Blois castle had no means of defending itself, the Duke immediately resolved to transfer the court to Amboise, to which Conde and Coligne were then invited. La Renaudie pursued his adventurous plot. The attack could still succeed because there were accomplices in the palace but he made the mistake of only carrying it out on the 17th March... On the 15th, March, Charles de Castelnau and thirty others of his followers were caught redhanded in the fortress of Noizay and laid down their arms without any guarantee of safe conduct. On the 17th, de la Rochechaudieu's men arrived too late on the battlements and they were defeated by the garrison. They were pursued through the woods and all those captured brought back to Amboise and thrown into the dungeons. La Renaudie tried to defend himself in the forest of Chateaurenaud and he was killed by a bullet from a harquebus. The repression was merciless. After a summary judgement of Captains Castelnau and Villemongis, they died on the scaffold. Others were tortured, hung drawn and quartered, thrown into the Loire with their hands and feet tied together or hanged from the castle's battlements. The gallery of the king's residence was thenceforth named "balcony for the hangings"... The young and beautiful Mary Stuart, wife of Francis II, cannot have failed to realize that one day in England she would be imprisoned for being a Catholic on the order of her cousin Elizabeth and later executed.
Amboise, which had been the scene of this terrible massacre, was abandoned for a while by the court. Thirty years later the leaders of the two parties met there once again to try and put out the fires of the Civil War. The treaty drawn up between the Catholics and the Protestants was an illusory agreement. A little after the Amboise peacemaking the fighting broke out again just as violently and when it was finished Henry IV's reign of union began. He assembled in Paris all those who made up his government, his entire court and most of the great artists. From now on the era of the Loire castles had come to an end.

From the XIIIth century

Louis XIII only came to Amboise to organize hunting parties in its beautiful forest between the Loire and the Cher. In the forest he would make his own meals of an onion omelette washed down with two glasses of wine. During the Fronde, Anne of Austria, Louis XIV and their followers took refuge in the castle. The governor of Amboise was le Blanc de la Valliere, whose daughter one day would be the lover of the young king. After Louis XIV came to power, Versailles became the palace of the absolute monarchy. Amboise was a mere place of exile for noteworthy prisoners. Superintendent Fouquet who had been accused of embezzlement was sent there under a heavy guard. The Count of Lauzun who had seduced "la Grande Mademoiselle" spent a certain time there before being given the right to return to the court.
In 1762 the Duke of Choiseul, Louis XV's prime minister, exchanged the land of Pompadour in Perigord for the baronial domain of Amboise but his aim was to make one of the finest castles of his time out of nearby Chanteloup. It was to this castle that he retired after he had fallen into disgrace. In 1785 the Duke of Penthievre bought Amboise. It was the eve of the Revolution. The former palace, the fortress of the royal family, was needless to say confiscated. Under the Empire, it fell into such disrepair that Napoleon got rid of it by giving it to Roger Ducos, who was an ex-regicide ex-consul who had lent his assistance on the event of the coup d'etat on 18 Brumaire. In order to avoid costly repairs, Ducos destroyed some of the building. At the Restoration, the Orleans family once again took over possession of the castle. In 1848 the king's residence was used as a place of detention for Emir Abd el Kader until Napoleon III decided to free him.

6 - Period bedroom
7 - State Chamber
8 - The Clos Lucé - Leonardo da Vinci's home and self-portrait

9

Angers

A castle Stronghold and the palace of King Rene

Built by Count Foulques Nerra, the first castle of Angers was then rebuilt under the orders of Saint Louis between 1228 and 1238. This austere citadel which dominates the River Maine is made up of a vast pentagon flanked with seven towers circled with white and black which surround enormous moats. Angers is still one of the most impressive examples of military art of the Middle Ages. It recalls the troubled times where it was advisable to be well protected against sudden attacks. But despite these appearances, the castle was the residence of a happy, strange and motley court where there were of course Angevins, but also people from Lorraine, Provence, Italians and Moors. Here lived Rene, King of Sicily and Jerusalem and Prince of Anjou: a poet and a builder, a devotee of literature and the arts, protector of the humble and the poor. During his reign a number of houses in the capital were rebuilt at his expense to shelter the poorest of his subjects, and the castle of Angers enjoyed its heyday. In 1466 a nobleman from Bohemia, Leon de Rosmithal, and his entourage were astonished, as his secretary wrote, to see that ''nowhere can there be seen a better equipped or stronger citadel. Inside we were treated with due respect and kindness. We were shown birds of every type. I've never anywhere else set eyes upon such beautiful menageries and aviaries where many birds, many of them quite unknown, could be seen flying. We saw Arab dogs brought from the furthest lands of the universe''.

A great lover of spectacle, Rene of Anjou put on mystery plays and organized tournaments. By reading the book which he wrote on tournaments, we can image the magnificence of the celebrations which took place at this time. Illuminated manuscripts show us pictures of woven tapestries and garlands of knights wearing their richest armour, of elegantly clad ladies watching from the stands, of people disguised as legendary heroes. If certain objectors disliked the luxury of these events, the merchants delighted in them. Whatever cost two ecus they sold at six, whether it be silk material or precious furs, because whenever a celebration was announced the women and the girls wanted to clothe themselves in the finest materials and the rarest jewels.

King Rene certainly liked festivities and fine colours - he wrote letters in gold with his own and enjoyed illuminating his own manuscripts. But this courteous and debonair man also liked studying, dreaming, the peaceful life, manual work and withdrawing into the fields. He wrote stories, composed music, painted and surrounded himself with artists whom he never left idle.

The Angevin XVth century, with the ephemeral reign of its last prince, seems to have been drawn from a fairy tale, then the following century was one of bitter memories. The wars of religion gave way to the most bloody combats and the savagest massacres. In 1585 Henry III ordered the castle of Angers to be demolished. Fortunately this order was only partly carried out. Only the battlements were knocked down and the height of the towers was reduced.

10

In 1598 Henri IV made a visit which saw the end of the violence and the pillaging perpetrated by the warring armies. A man endowed with luck and tenaciousness, King Henry IV had come to discuss peace with the Duke of Mercoeur, who was the leading chief in the West. At the castle, the engagement of Cesar of Vendome, son of Gabrielle of Estrees and Henry IV, to de Mercoeur's daughter was celebrated. Before returning to Paris, he signed the famous Edict of Nantes which proposed a just solution to both parties.

9 - The castle and the moast
10 - The Apocalyptic tapestries
11 - The castle and the gardens

12 - Azay le Rideau - The castle

13 - Filley de la Barre Chamber, around 1700

14 - Renaissance bedchamber

15 - Reflection of the castle in the Indre

Azay le Rideau

One of the finest achievements of the early Renaissance

On the right bank of the river Indre there used to be a castle named after Hugues Ridel or Rideau, a Banneret knight from Touraine under Philip Augustus. At the end of the Hundred Years war, the castle had a Burgundian garrison; it was besieged by partisans of the Dauphin Charles who massacred the defenders and burnt it to the ground. In the XVI century, Azay was in ruins. When Jean Berthelot, advisor to the king and master accountant, and Mayor of Tours, decided to rebuild it on an island in the river, it entailed much work and ingenuity. He entrusted the work to Etienne Rousseau, his master mason. Before building, the water which had seeped in the furrows of the foundations had to be drained and piles to be sunk. This exquisite manor house, which so harmoniously unites medieval architectural features with Italian influences, was very much the work of the beautiful Philippe (with her man's name), wife of Jean Berthelot. She carefully supervised the work, along with her confidant Guillaume Artau, parish priest of Saint-Cyr.

As with a number of castles of the period, Azay was not entirely completed. In 1527 Semblançay was sentenced to death and hanged at Montfaucon. This led to the ruin of his first cousin Berthelot. To avoid the same fate, he sought refuge in Metz, then a free town of the Empire. Francis I confiscated the property and made a gift of it to his captain of the guard, Antoine Raffin, named Poton, one of Francis' companions in arms at Marignan and Pavia. In the XVII century, Azay belonged to Henri of Beringhen, a faithful servant of Louis XIII and XIV, and at the end of the XVIII century to the beginning of the Third Republic, the castle belonged to the Biencourt family. In 1871 Prince Frederic Charles of Prussia lived in the castle with his military command. One day a chandelier crashed down on to his dinner table and he was convinced that it was in attempt on his life. He was barely restrained from burning down one of the finest works of art of the Renaissance. Today the blue rooves and dazzling stones of Azay are mirrored in the emerald waters of the Loire. For those who discover it, it remains the same as in Balzac's description: "Climbing over a hilltop, I looked down for the first time on this elaborately cut diamond, set in the river Indre and mounted on foundations decked with flowers".

16 - Francis 1st's facade

Blois

A composite mixture of many architectural styles. A palace which became one of the most famous in French history.

Blois was the capital of an old and powerful count. The castle was bought in the XIV century by Duke Louis of Orleans, brother of Charles VI. His son Dunois ensured that the castle was to remain one of the most important positions on the Loire valley during Charles of Orleans' captivity. The latter had been taken prisoner at the battle of Azincourt. After 25 years spent in England, this poet prince had only one desire, and that was repose.

"Peace is a treasure that cannot be too highly praised
My hatred of war will never be erased"

Blois was his oasis. He enjoyed transforming his residence. But his means were limited. His son Louis XII, became king of France and in full agreement with his wife Anne of Bretagne, decided to build a new wing. It would be decorated and fitted out as was Amboise. Francois of Pontbriant was appointed to direct the work. Simonet Guischard was in charge of the site. The main constructor was Colin Biart. This building, where the decorated gothic harmonises perfectly with the Italian taste for ornament, is one of the most remarkable creations of the French Renaissance. The red brick, white stone and blue slate combine to create the most attractive ensemble of colours. The collonaded gallery, where the royal porcupines are sculpted, and the gateway, over which the crowned Louis XII rides, remind us of the last ceremonies of the days of chivalry. But the king was a man concerned for his own comfort. His main objective was to have a pleasant home. Fine furniture, magnificent tapestries, gold and silver services from Nantes and Amboise were all brought to Blois. The first years of Princess Claude Francis I's future wife, were spent in this palace.

A virtuous court amidst fine gardens

For the people of western France, Queen Anne remained "duchess Anne". She was the kind-hearted duchess "whose breast was filled with pity for her Breton people" and "the duchess in clogs". Reality belies the myth. Anne was honest, virtuous, serious and pious but she also liked festivity. Her closest entourage included more than 300 people including a guard of 100 Breton gentlemen, 59 ladies and maids in waiting, 4 almoners, 7 chaplains, plus doctors, apothecaries and pages. She was particularly attentive to her female entourage. "La Cordelieve" was her own order of chivalry, to reward the most meritworthy of her ladies. The most important lords of the kingdom and even foreign princes requested the hands of the Queen's ladies in waiting in marriage. At Blois, everything was as magnificent as possible. The palace gardens were among the finest in France. The gardeners had mastered the art of weaving with living flowers and they would thread sumptous carpets made up of the heraldic colours. They would glisten in the sunshine, surrounding the ecu with the three fleurs de lys stamped with the royal diadem. At the royal table, the most exotic food was served: fish from the Loire, game from the dense local forests. The meals were cooked by the most reputed cooks in the kingdom, and accompanied with a liberal dose of Burgundy wine.

Anne died on 9th January 1514. The grief was widespread when the heralds in arms announced the terrible news in the streets of Blois. "Honourable and devout persons, pray to God for the soul of the noble, powerful and debonair Princess Anne, Queen of France. Say your pater nosters that God show her mercy".

Under Francis I

After the death of Louis XII, Francis I often stayed in Blois. The castle was the favourite residence of Queen Claude and her six children. As the court grew, the King carried out major building work. His entourage took up residence on the first floor of the new palace. The King reserved the second floor for himself. The stairway attributed to Dominique of Cortone, the niches where delicate statues of women look onto the old stones, or the salamander - emblem of the chevalier king - all hark back to this festive time.

Here the court poet Marot, and Clouet, the admirable portrait painter, Pierre Lescot the architect and sculptor, and the famous artists le Primatice, Della Robbia and Benvenuto Cellini all lived here a while.
In the colonnaded gallery, on the strange stairways or in the courtyard between the glowing torches, one can always imagine the King as the night falls with his gentlemen, artist friends and the beautiful and honest ladies of days gone by. Dressed in precious materials they became more and more numerous in the receptions, hunting parties, tournaments and other spectacles which dazzled the whole of Europe in their magnificence. But the great King Francis was conquered in Pavia in 1525, and he spent a year in Spain as a prisoner. On his return he abandoned Blois.

The wars of religion

During the wars of religion Queen Catherine of Medici, the widow of Henry II, had not the slightest desire to see her court entourage reduced. Receptions that she organized in the castles of the Loire were the meeting ground of Catholics and Protestants. Here she would attempt to reconcile them. In Blois Admiral de Coligny came to introduce her to his new wife. He was received with the greatest respect. Jeanne d'Albret, Queen of Navarre, signed the marriage contract of her son Henry with Margaret of France, sister of King Charles IX, in Blois. But the happy court of Francis I had become a den of intrigue. Queen Catherine used all the charm with which she and her ladies-in-waiting were endowed to foil these plots. Often after an impressive display of some kind there would be arrests, death sentences, or tragic vendetta killings between merciless adversaries. Then there was the night of Saint Barthelemy. After these massacres the provincial castles were abandoned for three years.
The court's return to Blois marked a change in the body politic decided on by Henry III. The first change of this kind took place in 1576 and the second in 1788. On this date the king retired first to Chartres and then to Blois as Charles VII had retired to Bourges, abandoning Paris to the enigmatic and fearless Henry de Guise le Balafre, head of la Ligue, who was conspiring his defeat. Henry III wanted to save his crown, reestablish peace and carry out judicious reforms. His inaugural speech from within the monarchy room was the speech of a king once again becoming conscious of the role which he should have assumed from the moment he came into power. But it was too late. The Duke de Guise, who had immense public support, whipped up popular feelings. Henry III decided to defend himself. It was then that Blois was to go through its darkest hours.

A test of strength: the terrible end of Balafre

On the 17 December 1588, during a dinner, Cardinal de Guise — who according to the Pope himself had nothing about him of a cardinal except his hat — raised his glass, looking at his brother, saying "I am drinking the health of the King of France". In his eyes, Henry III was already eliminated. The glorious, popular Duke de Guise, head of la Ligue must have seemed all powerful. But Henry III had been warned of the plot which was being hatched. Soon he had taken the necessary decision. Since he was not able to try le Balafre legally, he ordered his execution.
Early in the morning on the 23 December King Henry III requested to see the Duke de Guise and the cardinal. They were to meet him in council to discuss important business. At an early hour Guise arrived at the castle, where he waited in the anti-chamber with Aumont, Rambouillet d'O, his brother the cardinal, Gondi, the cardinal of Vendome and Montholon, the Keeper of the Seal. Since the previous evening le Balafre had received a number of warnings that a plot was being hatched against him, but as l'Estoile wrote "he could hardly believe that the king could or should want to play a nasty trick on him because his lofty spirit blinded

17 - Statue of Louis XII on horseback
18 - Renaissance Francis 1st staircase

him to the most obvious things. God had blindfolded him as He blindfolds those he wants to chastise and punish''.
As he was walking towards the king's cabinet ten or twelve men who had been waiting in ambush behind a tapestry jumped out and grabbed him by the arms and legs and stabbed him. They massacred him and his men, who cried out quite clearly ''My God, I am dying. Have pity on me. My sins are the cause''. The Duke himself was supposed to have cried ''Ah, gentlemen, what treachery!''. Du Gast dealt him the final blow. The king appeared, and on seeing him lying there dead he watched his face for a little while and said out loud: My God, how great he is; he seems even greater dead than alive''.
Cardinal de Guise had stayed in the council and heard the voice of his brother crying to God for mercy while the dagger and knife blows were raining down. He moved his chair to get up, saying ''they are killing my brother''. He was prevented from moving and along with the archbishop of Nyon he was taken prisoner and thrown into a cell where they remained without a fire to burn or seats to sit on. Twenty-four hours later Henry III had him executed. Four men pretending to lead him to the king murdered him with daggers and halbards.
On the evening of the same day the bodies of Balafre and the cardinal were cut into pieces in a dungeon of the castle and then burnt to ashes, which were thrown to the winds so that there would be neither relic nor memory of either of them.
Twelve days later Queen Catherine died in one of the castle rooms. The king himself finally breathed his last beneath the blows delivered by Jacques Clement on 2 August 1589.

19

20

For Blois the days of conspiracies and intrigues were not yet finished: Gaston of Orleans, brother of Louis XIII, hatched his plots in Blois. He left his accomplices to carry these out, with his typical cowardliness. Maria of Medici, exiled by her son, Louis XIII, didn't hesitate to slide out of a window to escape from the castle and managed to flee thanks to the darkness of the night... At court everyone was dumbfounded. Richelieu negotiated the reconciliation of the king and his mother, who was then offered the government of Anjou.
Later on, Blois was where Gaston of Orleans had to live his exile. He wanted to rebuild the castle, which he planned to knock down. Luckily he didn't have enough money. He is, however, responsible for creating the south-west wing, and the architect was the famous Mansart.
In 1668 Louis XIV, returning from Chambord, gave a sumptuous reception at the castle of Blois. After this the castle was abandoned. It was pillaged and damaged during the Revolution, and was restored in the course of the XIXth century.

19 - Room containing secret cabinets
20 - Catherine of Medici's chamber
21 - The south-facing facade (XVIIIth century)
22 - The Guard Room - XVIIth century ceiling XVIthe century Flemish tapestries

Brissac

Luxurious and grandiose

In 1492 Rene de Cosse possessed the estate of Brissac. The property was captured and then recaptured during the wars of religion and left half in ruins, before being transformed and rebuilt in the main between 1614 and 1621 by Jacques Corbineau for Charles II of Cosse, Duke of Brissac and Marshal of France, whose name has remained famous because he opened the gates of Paris to Henry IV. Between the two old medieval towers, the architect managed to insert the luxurious building which hangs over them. On the 12th August 1620, after the defeat of the rebel troups holding the bridges of Ce, Louis XIII made peace with his mother near Brissac. This magnificent castle has always belonged to the same family; one of the finest among French nobility: it produced 7 marshals, 5 governors of Paris, a Grand Master of Artillery and many other illustrious personalities.

23 - *Chambord - The Castle* 24 - *The Picture Gallery* 25 - *Francis 1st's Chamber*

old towns, wondered at all the kinds of magic and poetry, all the madnesses represented in the admirable fantasy of this fairyland chevalier castle.
Chambord has 440 rooms, 365 chimneys, 800 cornices and 15 staircases. It is in fact the palace of a dream come true. This colossal home outdoes all the other castles of the Loire in magnificence and symbolizes the explosive energy of a great reign, but over and above all its main purpose was as a meeting place for going hunting and as a palacial setting for sumptuous festivity. Although it could have housed a crowd of courtisans, the king only visited it from time to time. When he decided to spend a few days in Chambord with his second wife Eleanor and his pretty court favourite Anne d'Heuilly, Duchess of Etampes, the rooms that his suite were going to occupy were simply made inhabitable for the occasion. The king would walk with his courtesans, his artists and his fine friends through the gardens. The gardeners wove sumptuous carpets of ardent colours in flowers, to represent the three golden lilies on a blue background, the royal diadem or the salamander on a bed of tongues of fire. The flower beds were overflowing with flowers and the mirrors of water in which the sky was reflected, the gushing fountains and the pleasure gardens all seemed made to illustrate Rabelais' passage where he describes the famous abbey of Theleme. The sumptuous setting required by Francis I was made for people of high society who enjoyed the continual assuaging of their desires for an enchanting life.
In the French court the role of women became more and more important. Francis I would say "a court without women is like a year without Spring, and a Spring without roses". The number of ladies in the court had considerably increased; the king's house had 27 ladies and the queen's retinue counted many more. The presents given them were expensive but "the king was not considered a miser in that particular field". The king loved women: Brantome tells us that "although he held the opinion that they were highly inconstant and variable, he would never hear anything said against them in his court and required that they should be shown every honour and respect".
The finest feast thrown by the king marked the arrival of Charles V of Spain during the Winter of 1539. Francis bore no bitterness towards his previous enemy. On the contrary, he wanted to impress him. He wanted him to visit the finest of the Loire castles; Amboise, Blois and above all Chambord. To mark the occasion the Baron of Montmorency — a Grand Master of Ceremonies — had furnished the main rooms very lavishly. They were covered with tapestries and decorated with objets d'art.

The emperor admired Chambord "as if it were the essence of what human industry can achieve". He spent a few days there, hunting deer and living in one of the finest and most fertile parts of France".

In the Autumn of 1545 the king, who had suddenly aged, wrote these two lines with a diamond tip on a window pane;

> Women often change
> Woe to he who trusts them

which are often reproduced with a variation;

> Women often change
> Mad is he who trusts them

Later on, Louis XIV came to Chambord. This is where Moliere created "Monsieur de Pourceaugnac" and "le Bourgeois Gentilhomme". In the XVIIIth century the good king Stanislas of Poland and his wife consoled themselves for the loss of their kingdom by accepting the hospitality of their relations. After them Marshal Maurice of Saxe, winner of the Battle of Fontenoy, was given Chambord by Louis XV and the right to keep the Saxe Cavalry regiment mobilized near him. One brigade of this regiment was composed of blacks from Senegal mounted on white horses. In the refurnished castle (undertaken by the king) the marshal lived an uninhibited and dissolute life for a few years.

Under the empire, Berthier, Prince of Wagram, took possession of Chambord.

During the Restoration, the palace, marked with the memory of so many kingly celebrations, was put up for sale. It was bought back by national subscription and offered to the young Duke of Bordeaux, who took its name. The Count of Chambord, the last legitimate claimant to the throne of France, left the magnificent property to the Bourbon Parme. Today it belongs to the French state.

Chambord is particularly reminiscent of a grandiose reign. It reminds us of Marignan, the concordat of Bologne, the Perpetual Peace with the Swiss, who ever since have come to serve in the French armies. As we look upon this building, still intact, we would hardly be surprised to see a few Swiss guards at attention in the gardens, with their steel breast plates, their long pikes and their short swords.

27 - Sunrise over the castle
28 - Chimney details
29 - Sound and light
30 - The main, double-spiral staircase

Cinq Mars and Luynes

A fine past of which the only remains are ruins and a beutiful and strong fortress

These two estates, very close to each other, bear the names of two gentlemen who were favourites of Louis XIII. But their destinies were very different.
Henry d'Effiat, Marquis of Cinq Mars, was born in the first. In 1642 Gaston of Orleans, the king's brother, had lured him into a conspiracy and paid for his rashness with his life and was decapitated at the age of 22. On Richelieu's order the castle was rased to the ground, "to the height of infamy". Two large towers with their gothic rooms allow one still to imagine the importance and the architectural value of this old and feudal home.

The four towers of LUYNES dominate the peaceful valleys of the Loire and the Cher. Outside, the castle still has all the features of a fortress. Inside, the interior courtyard was remade by Hardouin de Maille. In 1619 the de Maille lands in Touraine were bought by Charles d'Albet de Luynes and Louis XIII made him a Duke with peerage under the name of Luynes. He was promoted from being hunting captain to high constable once he had rid the young king of his minister Concini. Charles de Luynes increased still further the prestige of his family by marrying the incomparable Marie de Rohan. This young, sixteen year old, blond girl, "a pretty and conversant lass", was to become the intransigent Duchess of Chevreuse. After this the Dukes of Luynes accumulated titles, important posts and gave France some of its most remarkable personalities.

Chateaudun

The Fief of brave Dunois

Thibaud the Cheat, greatest of the counts of Tours, built a fortress on a hill spur looking over the Loire valley. One of his successors added a large keep. It was sold to Louis d'Orleans by the last count of Blois. The former was the brother of Charles VI. Chateaudun then became part of Charles d'Orleans' estate; he offered it to his halfbrother John, bastard son of Orleans. The brave Dunois, legitimate son of Louis and Mariette of Enghin, built the new extensions. Others were built by Francis II d'Orlean Longeville, in the early Renaissance style.
The castle was burnt during the wars of religion and rebuilt by the architect Hardouin. Chateaudun later became part of the Luynes family property before being bought by the French government and restored.

31 - Cinq Mars - The Castle
32 - Luynes - The castle in Springtime
33 - Reflections of the castle in the Loir

Chaumont

The revolutionary little court of Madame de Stael

From behind the loopholes in its massive walls, Chaumont seems to be watching over the river. Proudly dominating the Loire and always harking back to the power of the house of Amboise, the castle projects its medieval outline on to the river. Louis XI had pulled it down to punish the local landlord, but once they had returned into favour, Charles I of Amooise and then his son rebuilt their formidable castle. After the death of her husband, Catherine de Medici took Chenonceau from Diane of Poitiers and offered her Chaumont in compensation. The estate belonged successively to La Tour d'Auvergne, Viscount of Turenne — father of the famous Turenne —, to Charles of Beauvillier, duke of Saint Aignan, tax collector to the duke of Burgundy, and to Jacques le Ray who set up a pottery manufacture directed by the Italian Nini. During the Empire, Madame de Stael, exiled from Paris by Napoleon, came to live here. She surrounded herself with her admirers; liberals who were fighting the Empire, if only platonically: a mere salon opposition between the very walls which had known conspirators of a rougher stamp. Restored by the d'Aramon, then by the Broglie family, Chaumont was bought by the French government in 1938.

34 - The castle overtowering the Loire
35 - The inner courtyard
36 - The Amédée de Broglie stables (1877)

35

36

38

39

Chenonceau

The Famous Home of the Incomparable Diane

At the start of the XVI century along the edge of the river Cher, on a very attractive site, there was a fortified manor with a strange mill standing on strong pillars embedded in the granite river bed. The estate of Chenonceau had belonged to the Marques family from Auvergne since 1243. In 1512, one of his descendants, burdened by debt, sold their ancestral seat.

Thomas Bohier and Catherine Briconnet, his wife, - creators of the most charming mansion in Tourraine.

Thomas Bohier was financial officer for the province of Normandy and for a long time he had coveted Chenonceau. He bought all the buildings for 12500 pounds, then all the surrounding lands which became a lordship in 1512. Bohier was the nephew of Chancellor Duprat; his wife Catherine Briconnet, from the Touraine, was the daughter of a minister of Charles VIII. Le Bohier, the Briconnet and their relations, the La Baume Semblancay, all held lucrative positions of responsibility. Thomas dreamed of having a country castle. The Manor of the Marques, with its feudal battlements, no longer matched the new style of living. Only the keep of this austere building was kept on. The rest was rebuilt or renewed, and instead of the mill anchored in the river Cher, an early Renaissance style square house appeared with merely ornamental towers, battlements and machicolations.
The new Chenonceau was the fruit of the imagination of Thomas Bohier and, more particularly, of his wife Catherine whom he left to watch over the building work when his duties took him to Italy with the king to administer the finances of the "Milanais" and as munitioner to the army.
In 1521, Cardinal Antoine Bohier, Archbishop of Bourges, came to consecrate the castle chapel. Francis I had given permission for a bridge to be built over the Cher. Attracted by the ease of life in Touraine, and sensitive to beauty in all its forms, the king had come to admire the property. He declared that it was "a fine and pleasant site and house bridging the river Cher in a most beautiful part of the country".
Bohier died in Italy on the 14 March 1524 and Catherine only survived him by two years. Their son Antoine inherited the charming home. However, Francis I had not forgotten his visit. He undertook a close examination of his former treasurer's accounts. To his great surprise, Antoine Bohier was ordered to repay enormous sums to the government. In 1533, an arrangement was made to prevent him from falling into complete ruin. The king would let him off his fine in exchange for Chenonceaux. The Counstable of Montmorency came to take possession of the estate in Francis' name. The latter announced his imminent arrival...

After becoming a royal lordship, the castle of Catherine Bohier was to receive one of the court's most beautiful "Huntresses".

The king enjoyed coming on hunting parties with Queen Elenora at Chenonceau, in other words with his closest relation and a few of his closest friends. Apart from his son the dauphin Henry and his beautiful daughter Catherine of Medici, two ravishingly attractive women held very important places among the courtiers who would accompany the king on his trips to the provinces. There was Anne of Pisseleu, Lady of Heuilly, Duchess of Etampes, his favourite, and Diane de Saint Vallier of Poitiers, widow of Louis de Breze, Senechal of Normandy, with whom the dauphin was passionately in love.
During the day, the hunters and huntresses pursued the deer in the tall woods. The Duchess of Etampes, the Florentine Catherine and Diane of Poitiers were all intrepid amazons. When dusk came down, the castle would glitter with light; revels, masked balls and torchlit dances threw glowing reflections on the calm waters of the Cher, which provided the perfect backdrop to this fairyland setting. Poetry was read and madrigals written, for it was an ideal of the times to be both strong and cultured. Nevertheless, Madame d'Etampes despised Diane of Poitiers, a seductress whose appearance was somewhat chilling but whose fortunes were improving. Catherine hated this beautiful widow, the mistress of Henry, even more; he was nineteen years younger than her. Diane's enemies claimed that she had already surrendered herself to Francis I, in order to obtain a pardon for her father Saint Vallier, who was accused of treason. This was sheer slander. What was certainly true, however, was that her fortunes were improving... The young prince invariably dressed in black and white, the colours of his "Dame". His emblem was Diane's crescent moon.

Henry II gives Chenonceau to his favourite

On the 31 March, 1547, king Francis I died in Rambouillet. Henry had his wife Catherine annointed at Saint Denis; during the ceremony, Diane took a place on the stand reserved for the royalty, and the new monarch decided that no better gift could be offered her than that of Chenonceau. From 1535, the estate had been government property, and as such could not be given away, according to a royal edict of 30 June 1539. To get round this difficulty, Henry referred in the donation deeds to the eminent services of the late Senechal, Louis of Breze. Henry declared that by granting his widow the rewards that he could have hoped for during his lifetime, he would be repairing an injustice. The royal lover offered Diane diamonds, crown pearls and enormous sums of money, much of a national 20 pound bell tax also came Diane's way. Rabelais dared refer to this by writing, "the king has hung all the bells in the kingdom around the neck of his mare".

Diane's reign

Diane, though wealthy in financial and material terms, wished to increase her fortune, and began by putting her lands in order, managing and harnessing them to serve her interests. She wanted to turn Chenonceau into a domain that could vie with the finest royal palaces.
To achieve this, a lavish garden was essential. It would provide a harmonious complement to the castle. In 1551, she arranged the two-hectare garden, watered by the La Roche fountain. Lawns, a fish hatchery, a vegetable garden and an orchard began to appear. Diane loved flowers. She was presented with gifts of rosetrees, melons and artichokes - very rare at the time. Gardeners, hoticulturers, designers and architects all worked hand in hand in seeking a perfect union between nature and the castle. In 1556, Philibert Delorme carried out tests on the riverbed. Diane commissioned him to build the famous bridge linking the grand mansion to the woody hedges and fountains, like a meadow in April, on the opposite bank.

Thus embellished, Chenonceau became one of the main court residences. Diane was happy to play the sovereign in it where she supported the Catholic Guise against the protestant Condes and Colignys. Henry spent one in every three days with his "perfect friend". The bewitching beauty of this woman who had no scruples about being painted naked astride a deer was magically maintained; she dazzled everyone...

The sobriety of her clothing perfectly matched her noble bearing and highlighted the milky whiteness of her skin. To offset the effects of age, she employed a few simple recipes. In summer and winter alike she would rise and take a bath in freezing cold water. She would then go riding, to return and go back to bed until twelve noon. She never used make-up. Moreover, she behaved with an intelligent coquetterie, astuteness, reserve and pride. All of this had the desired effect on the king. He plied her with the most precious gifts. Appointed Duchess of Valentences, Chatelaine of Anet and Chenonceau the "plus belle des belles" could have continued playing the central role if Henry's passion for tournaments had not brought him misfortune. In the spring of 1559, he celebrated the marriages of his daughter and sister with a jousting tournament. He wanted to take on Gabriel of Montgomery, in the name of his lady. Accidentally wounded, he died a few days later in the Toúrnelles palace.

The queen's revenge

Diane's reign had come to an end. Queen Catherine took over the government of her country. The legitimate wife, so long humiliated by the favourite, demanded that she return the crown jewels and the castle of Chenonceau. Diane attempted to resist, but Catherine made it understood that she was prepared to use armed

37 - The Castle and the gardens
38 - The Catherine of Medici garden
39 - The Diane of Poitiers garden
40 - The Marques Tower - Renaissance facade

force... Intimidated, the lady of Chenonceau was stripped of her jewels and her enchanting domain.
In return, Catherine gave her Chaumont. For the haughty duchess, Chaumont was no replacement for Chenonceau. She preferred to withdraw to her castle at Anet. She died there at the age of 66, as beautiful as ever.

The favourite residence of Catherine and her court

Catherine was often compared in poetry to June, goddess of the family; she was very glad to take up residence in the estate where her rival had lived for so long on power and insolent beauty. To mark her victory in a spectacular manner she offered a magnificent reception at Chenonceau. It was in honour of her son king Francis II and his young wife Mary Stuart. The procession went by under a triumphal archway decorated with the coats of arms of France, Scotland and the Medici. Primatice had designed the costumes for the lavish ball that followed.
Despite the merciless civil war between Catholics and Protestants, Chenonceau, once more within the royal fold, became the backdrop to Saturnalia as yet unparallelled. A few years later, the Queen decided to extend the building. She used the transformation plan recommended by Philibert Delorme, who had died in 1570. She commissioned a two-floor gallery to be built over the arches of the bridge over the Cher. From 1580 to 1585, the architect Androuet du Cerceau constructed this part of the building. With its classical severity, it was designed for royal meals and receptions.
Like her former rival, Catherine loved gardens. Like Lorenzo of Medici who had planted rare blooms around his palace, she sent for foreign plants and even set up a silk-weaving workshop in the park as well as a hen-coop and a menagerie of bizarre animals.
It is well known that the Queen ruled on behalf of her sons Francis II, Charles IX and Henry III. Despite her many and permanent worries, she managed to find the time to organise hunting parties, jousting on the river, balls and other entertainments. It is true that to serve the needs of her policies and to be kept abreast of everything that transpired, the queen sometimes used unconventional methods. Her body of spies was composed of a certain number of girls of noble birth, carefully selected and trained. They were known as the ''Flying squadron''. Ronsard in his sonnets, ballads and madrigals sung the charm of these ''honnetes demoiselles'' who, depending on the time of the day wore gold or silver dresses. It was as if they were clad in the garments of either the sun or the moon. Brantome described the court of queen Catherine as a real earthly paradise and a school of all honesty, but he often contradicts this by describing the dishonesty, intrigues, vendettas and sensual excesses of its dramatis personae. Sometimes, to reward a devout servant or to reveal the roots of a conspiracy, Catherine would oblige her ladies in waiting to prostitute themselves. During the parties on the banks of the river, and in the woods, bachic festivities often led to manifold excesses. The beautiful ladies of the flying squadron were the nymphs and sirens, pursued by the court satyrs...

Strange celebrations

In 1577, Catherine arranged a reception at Chenonceau to celebrate the arrival of her son Henry III, back from Poland to succede to his brother Charles IX. The table had been laid behind the Tour de Marques, near the rock fountain. Henry had dressed up as a woman for the occasion and was sporting a corset encrusted with diamonds and fine pearls. He was surrounded by his ''minions'' - Gondi, Saint Luc, Joyeuse, Saint Megrin...
Queen Catherine, Queen Margaret of Navarra — wife of the future Henry IV — and the reigning Queen Louise of Vaudemont presided over the banquet.
Young women from the court, naked to the waist, served the meal. Their hair was cut short like that of newly married women. They were all dressed in dual-colour damask mens' clothes. The soiree ended with a fireworks show in the grounds, along the river banks and in punts. Pierre d'Estoile recounts in his journal that

this Chenonceau banquet cost more than 100000 pounds; it was paid for on a loan raised among "the king's most faithful servants" and several Italians who made sure they were repayed twofold.
The last Valois faced the destiny which was cutting down his race by living in unparallelled luxury. However, the civil war was growing fiercer every day. The Queen mother was never short of a plan to save her most beloved son. The duke of Guise, head of the Ligue, was beheaded and this increased the king's unpopularity. Catherine died in the castle of Blois. Before her death, she entrusted Chenonceau to Louise of Vaudemont, her daughter-in-law. A little later, Henry III was murdured by the mad Jacques Clement.

The "White Lady" of Chenonceau

Queen Louise had inherited Chenonceau, and her first concern was to protect her domain and her vassals. From the 1 February 1589, she wrote to Gilles of Faverolles, captain of 200 armed men, to ensure that no violence was carried out on her estate. When informed of the king's death, she was struck with remorse. This pious and discreet princess had never ceased to love her husband. Six months later, she arrived at Chenonceau and shut herself aways in silence, alone with her memories. In this castle designed for enjoying life, clack draperies inlaid with silver tears were stretched over the wooden panelling of her room. Where gentlemen and ladies had danced the galliard and the waltz to the light of fireworks displays, now Ursuline nuns came to meditate at this near-monasterial retreat, along with the Queen.
Up to her death in 1601, Henry III's widow only found repose from her incurable remorse in prayer, solitude and tireless generosity towards all the poor in the country. In her haustere dwelling, her bright outline stood out, for Louise had adopted the tradition of mourning in white. She was known as the "White lady of Chenonceau"; of all women who have lived in this fairyland castle, she, doubtless, was the best symbol of the most genuine love.

Changing Times

The castle of Chenonceau had been coveted for so long... The Bohier family took it from the Marques because this small manor belonging to these ruined nobles was situated in an enchanting setting; Francis I took it from the Bohier, after they had extended it, and Henry II gave it as a present to his lover; then Catherine replaced Diane, and so on...
But with the reign of Henry IV, the days of the Touraine castles had come to an end. The Bearnais who had imposed their royal authority with such difficulty and moved the seat of government back to Paris, had been unwise in leaving the capital. Queen Louise left Chenonceau to her niece, Francoise of Mercour, married to Cesar, Duke of Vendome.
The Vendome family and their successors the Bourbon Conde did not wish to invest large sums on a provincial residence, which they were not going to inhabit.

A salon of philosophy and pleasures of the rustic life

However, this refuge of gardens, river and bridges attracted Claude Dupin, a rich XVIII century farmer-general. In 1733, he bought the castle from the Duke of Bourbon. Madame Dupin, a charming and witty bourgeoise, attracted philosophers to her residence. The latter were only too happy to find accomodation in this form. Among this intellectual elite figured the great names of the age of Enlightenment.
There was Montesquieu, Buffon, Mably, Condillac, Voltaire, Madame de Tencin and Madame du Deffand. Jean-Jacques Rousseau became Mme. Dupin's secretary and taught her daughter. "One had such a fine time in this beautiful setting" he wrote "and there was such good cheer". I became as fat as a friar. «We played music, and acted dramas. I composed some lines entitled the "The avenue of Sylvie" after an avenue in the park looking on to the Cher». During his free time, the solitary dreamer revelled in the rustic life which he wanted to bring back into fashion. Under the shady trees, he completed the manuscript on "l'Emile" - his famous treatise on education.
The factitious calm of this period was followed by the great upheaval of the French Revolution. Miraculously, the castle which had witnessed the amourous intrigues of the most beautiful of the royal favourites and which was stamped with the trace of the most enigmatic queen in French history, survived intact. Madame Dupin, respected and loved by the villagers, died in 1799, aged 93. She was buried as she had wished in the Chenonceau grounds. In 1864, Madame Pelouze bought Chenonceau and restored the buildings to make them look as when originally designed. Some windows were filled in the cariatides which Catherine of Medici had put on the facades and some of the other ornamentation was relegated to the gardens. The Menier family has owned the castle since 1913.

44

45

41 - The castle floodlit
42 - The great gallery over the Cher
43 - Medicis chamber
44 - Madame Dupin welcoming Jean-Jacques Rousseau
45 - Henri II and Diane of Poitiers

Cheverny

The charm of the countryside highlights the beauty of this haughty and magnificent edifice

The splendid castle of Cheverny, sitting in the heart of woodland France, was built between 1606 and 1634. It belongs to the last period of the Loire valley lordships, when powerful aristocratic families extended the days of royal rule by putting up castles which contrasted in their scale and luxury with the small lodges of the provincial nobility, usually fairly poor. Henri Hurault, Count of Cherverny, was the son of Philip Hurault, Chancellor to King Henry III and IV, and first chancellor of the Order of the Holy Spirit. He wanted to acquire a personal mansion which would suit the status he and his family had attained, and would match his lavish tastes. He called upon the architect Boyer and the painter Jean Mosnier to bring his project to fruition. As with Chenonceau, the mistress of the castle directed the construction work. This lady of Cheverny was the second wife of the Count.

A husband thirsty for revenge

Henri Hurault, Count of Cheverny, married as his first wife Françoise de Chabot. One day king Henry IV made a horned cuckold sign, which the Count of Cheverny realised was directed at him (he caught sight of it in a mirror). He galloped straight off to his castle, arriving at five o'clock in the morning. One of his pages, who, to be sure, was not expecting his arrival, leapt out of the bedroom window of the mistress of the castle. In so doing he tripped and broke his leg. Cheverny slew him without a moment's hesitation. Then, with the same pitiless determination, he sent for a priest, entered his wife's bedroom, holding in one hand a goblet of poison, and a sword in the other.
The hapless wife chose the poison and expired. This all transpired in the early hours of the morning. Cheverny then rode back to Blois, arriving just as the king was going to bed. Henry IV learnt of these events, of which he was the prime cause, and could not hide his regret and dissatisfaction. He exiled the hard-hearted lord to the provinces, to Cheverny, to think things over. There he fell in

love with the daughter of his bailiff and offered her marriage. This woman turned out to be a person of great character; when the Count was once again accepted into the court in Paris, she managed the property with great skill. She made the greatest contribution to embellishing Cheverny.
Cheverny, built in the XVIIth century, is a castle of classical style. This focal point for hunting is one of the rare seats still lived in by the same family. Upon his death, the Marquess de Vibraye, a descendant of the Hurault family, bequeathed the property to his nephew and wife, the Viscount and Viscountess de Sigalas.

46 - Cheverny - The Castle
47 - The castle floodlit
48 - The King's chamber
49 - The small drawing-room Flemish tapestries

47

48

49

50 - The castle
The hunting party leaving on a hunt

52 - The goblin tapestry

51 - The Hunting Museum

53 - The Guard Room

52

53

Chinon

These grandiose ruins testify to one of the most moving moments in French history

Built on a cliff over the river Vienna, this castle was one of the main fortresses of the counts of Anjou and the kings of England. Henry Plantagenet died here in 1189. There were three castles separated by moats: Fort Saint George, the central fort and the Coudray fort. This formidable enclosure with its various towers was taken to be impregnable. When the future Charles VII was only the ''poor king of Bourges'' he is said to have chosen Chinon as his residence. He lived in the delightful residential section of the central fort.

Though damaged by time, Chinon is still one of the most precious remains of old France. Its striking ruins still convey the sentation of the fortress where the dauphin was protected from the English invader. In one of these upper rooms, Joan of Arc met him. From the top of these terraces, the heroic girl contemplated the landscape where all the virtues of the French land seemed to be condensed. Three months later, the ''King of Bourges'' became Charles the Victorious and went to Reims to be consecrated.

54 - The castle overtowering the Vienne
55 - Castle relics
56 - Room where Jean of Arc met Charles VII

55

56

Fontevraud

A famous abbey for women

Robert d'Arbrissel, a famous Breton monk and preacher, chose as the site for a future monastery a solitary wild valley not far from Saumur, near a brook known from time immemorial as the Fontaine d'Evrauld. He conferred the management of his monastery upon a woman, Petronille de Chemille. This wealthy abbey, with its huge estate, was consecrated in 1119 by Pope Calixtus II. It houses the tombs of King Henry II and his wife Elenora of Aquitaine, of their son Richard the Lionheart and of Isabelle of Angouleme, wife of King John. This earned him the name of the "Saint Denis of English Kings".
The rule of Robert d'Abrissel was very austere. Later, he abandoned his preliminary ideal. During the age of Louis XIV, the best known of his abbesses was Gabrielle Adelaide de Rochechouart-Mortemart, sister of La Montespan, who used to amaze visitors with the extent of her knowledge.
At the Revolution, the nuns of Fontevraud were dispersed. One of the most illustrious abbeys of Christendom became a house of detention.

57 - Overal view of the Abbey
58 - The Romanic Abbey kitchens

59

Fougères sur Bièvre

One of the last examples of feudal architecture

The first building here was a fortress. During the hundred years' war, the Black Prince partly destroyed these fortified buildings. In 1470, Pierre de Refuge, advisor to Charles of Orleans, then treasurer to Louis XI, rebuilt the walls of Fougeres and restored the strong keep. His cousin, Jean of Villebresme, completed the work. But Fougeres is still basically a military fortress. With its moats surrounding the machicolated bastions, it is strongly protected and belongs to the middle ages.

Langeais

The impregnable fortress and sumptuous dwelling of pleasure

Situated on the border of Anjou and Touraine, Langeais, with its peppercorn towers, battlements and moats seems collosal beside the vast river. This illustrious fortress still contains the remains of the first keep, built by the shady Foulques Nerra, who did not hesitate to burn his wife to death because he thought her unfaithful. Rebuilt by Saint Louis, Langeais was then owned by Pierre de la Brosse, favourite of Philippe the Hardy, who later came to grief on Montfaucon's gibet.
During the hundred years' war, an Anglo-Gascon garrison turned Langeais into a stronghold of defence.
After so many regrettable events, Louis XI rebuilt Langeais. He was not intimidated by his powerful partner, Duke Francois of Bretagne. He resolved to turn the castle into a strategic position to defend the Loire valley. To complete the project, which meant a great deal to him, he chose his friend Jean Bourré.
Jean Bourré was born at Chateau Gontier in 1424, to a poor family which had worked its way to the highest positions. He had been made a noble and become rich. He was appointed General of Finances and treasurer of France. He distinguished himself under Charles VIII, who valued his services. When travelling in Flanders and Italy, he had noticed the fine buildings to be found there and met the greatest painters of his day. This explains the dual aspect of Langeais: from the outside, it is the fortress commissioned by Louis XI, but, within its walls, there are small towers, mullioned windows and skylights, all of which herald the early Renaissance. The defensive features proved pointless when the marriage of the Duchess Anne to Charles VIII ended Breton independance. The

60

59 - Fougères sur Bièvre - The Castle
60 - Langeais - The Castle

SAUMUR
AUTOS

wedding took place in the main hall at Langeais. To mark the event, the castle was decorated with tapestries, imported from Turkey and Flanders. The most exquisite silver articles had been sent for from the royal palaces and gold and silk materials were everywhere to be seen. This marriage astonished the European courts, for the previous year, the heir of the Breton dukes had been married by proxy to Maximilien of Austria at Rennes.
The castle of Langeais now belongs to the Institut de France, to which it was bequeathed in 1904 by Jacques Siegfried.

61 - Langeais - The drawbridge
62 - The gardens - The inward-facing facade

63 - WEDDING OF CHARLES VIII WITH ANN OF BRITTANY - from left to right:
Pierre Bourreau Notary, Guillaume de Rochefort, Prince of Orange, Louis d'Orléans future Louis XII, Pierre de Beaujeu, Anne de Beaujeu, Charles VIII, Archbishop Bishop, Cardinal Georges d'Amboise, Ann of Brittany, Three Maids of Honor, Two Guards.

64 - The Chapel
65 - A XIIIth century shrine
66 - A gothic bed and a XVth century crédence
67 - The Virgin and Child by Duccio (XIIIth century)

68 - Loches - Medieval town

69 - The royal dwelling

Loches

Royal residence and sinister government prison: iron cages contrasting with the image of the beautiful Agnes Sorel

The old castle of the counts of Anjou which dominates the Indre on the north-east used to be an important fortress, which Philip Augustus and Richard the Lionheart fought over. In the XV century, Loches along with Chinon was one of the two most powerfully armed fortresses of the "poor king of Bourges" in the Loire valley. It was here that Joan of Arc managed to persuade him to leave for Reims. The heroine had just retaken Orleans and showed the authenticity of her mission through this victory.
In Loches, Charles VII, protected by a formidable army, occupied the pleasant residence. Despite the war which raged with its tales of heroism and atrocities, it was here that he lived the happiest years of his life, with the beautiful Agnes Sorel. This young girl was as intelligent as she was beautiful. She was the king's favourite after 1444, and lived in his residence, taking part in all official ceremonies. Charles gave her the castle of Beaute in Champagne, and the estate matched her beauty. We are indebted to her for having influenced the king to uphold men such as Jacques Coeur, Breze, Richemont, the most faithful supporters of the legitimate monarchy. If her luxurious life-style outraged many, (she loved precious stones silks from the east, and oriental gold cloth), she nevertheless was a devoted woman, who showed a sincere and tireless generosity to the poor. During the final days of her brief existence, the "belle des belles" left 2000 gold ecus and many other articles to Notre Dame college in Loches. She was buried in the sanctuary between the medieval fortress and the royal residence.
Louis XI turned Loches into a prison. It is common knowledge that his police were very brutal. The king would open prisons as his fancy took him. A few years later, Anne of Bretagne left the marvellous oratory built for her by Louis XII in this castle. In the sculpted stone can be seen speckles of ermine and finely engraved girdles at the site where the pious king would come to meditate in solitude. But Loches was nevertheless a state prison. Martelet was incarcerated in this prison as was Lodovico Il Moro, Duke of Milan, captured by the soldiers of Louis XII. He was firstly locked up in Lys Saint Georges castle in the Berry, then transferred to Loches after an attempted escape. To offset boredom, he covered his cell in paintings and inscriptions. One of them is moving in its simplicity: "He who is unhappy".

70 - St. Ours Church

71 - Portrait of Agnes Sorel

72 - The keep

73

74

Montsoreau

The hide-out of a terrible family

Montsoreau, which towers over the Loire, was built by Jean de Chambes, maître-d'hôtel to Charles VII. If, on the one hand, this charming castle often received illustrious pilgrims, heading for the abbey of Fontevraud, it was nonetheless known for the story of the "Dame de Montsoreau", of her husband and of her lover, the gallant Bussy, who was murdured a few leagues aways.

The revenge of Montsoreau

Charles de Chambes, Lord of Montsoreau, Master Hunter to the Duke of Alencon, an astute and versatile prince, not always a reliable friend, had married Francoise de Maridor in 1576. Bussy d'Amboise was the Duke's favourite, a seductive, handsome witty man who was known to read Plutarch. He was refined, imposing and extremely attractive to women. The day came when Bussy decided to add the pretty Countess of Montsoreau to the list of his conquests. Soon after he wrote "I have caught the master hunter's roe-deer in my net". The indiscreet and over-confident lover was to pay dearly for his boasting.
The Duke of Alencon had tired of his favourite. One day Alencon told Montsoreau about his wife's infidelity, adding that he was too concerned with the honour and the glory of his house to hide such an outrageous insult from him.
The husband arrived at Montsoreau in a fury. He brutally forced his terrified wife to write a letter arranging a rendez-vous with Captain Bussy. It was to take place in the castle of Coustanciere, near Saumur. Bussy and one chosen companion arrived at the agreed time. He entered the castle and the doors slammed behind him. A group of thugs moved forward to murder him. Bussy had ofter declared that "fear had never found a place in my heart". He was now to prove it. Sword in hand, he defended himself. Losing his sword, he grabbed tables, chairs, stools... When he saw that his end was near, he moved towards a window. He was preparating to jump when one of the killers felled him at the feet of his enemy.

Talcy

A medieval home

The Talcy estate in Blaisois was bought in 1517 by Bernard Salviati, a Florentine merchant who became Francis I's banker. He married Francoise Doucet, descended from a line of Masters of the Exchequer at Blois. Talcy was a mere fortress which they simply enlarged and embellished. Their son Jean received Catherine of Medici there in 1562, as well as Charles IX, Henry of Navarre and Conde in the hope that this meeting would create a lasting peace in the kingdom. The Salviati kept Talcy until 1667 and are still known of today thanks to two beautiful daughters in the family. Ronsard met the young Cassandre, daughter of Bernard Salviati, in 1545. He fell passionately in love with her. He wrote of this love in his odes and love poems. Aggripa d'Aubigne was deeply enamoured of Diane Salviati, the daughter of Jean, but the latter had not the slightest intention of allowing her to marry the austere and passionate Calvinist. He was opposed to the marriage, and, the ultimate misfortune for Aggripa, Diane died shortly after. The poet never forgot her.
Since 1932, the castle of Talcy has belonged to the French government.

73 - The Guard Room
74 - The facade overlooking the Loire
75 - Talcy - The Castle

77

Saumur

This castle, which appears under a blue sky in "Les Très Riches Heures du Duc de Berry" (the Duke of Berry's Hour-Book) was rebuilt at the end of the XIVth century by Louis 1st of Anjou, brother of Charles V. In the XVth century, René of Anjou had the interior arranged.
The imposing, brand new edifice "spread a great light when the sun shone upon it". René was passionately fond of festivities. In the tournaments which he held in SAUMUR, he gathered together the most valiant cavaliers. All those who stopped in the town were amazed at the beauty of its location and the festive atmosphere which reigned there.
In the XVIth and XVII th centuries, SAUMUR knew unequalled prosperity. The introduction of the reform, the radiance of the protestant academy and the establishing of several religious orders (Recollects, Capucins and Oratorians) made the town a radiant intellectual centre.
From 1552 to 1589, the violence committed during the religious warn finally led to a treaty which attributed the town to the protestants as a fortress.
DUPLESSIS-MORNAY, the "Huguenots' Pope", a great friend of Henri IV, became governor of this town which gave the protestants access to the Loire.
The repealing of the Edict of Nantes (1685) was fatal to the town's activity.
The riding school dates back to when a regiment of carabiniers came to Saumur in 1763.
The school was founded in 1771. Marshal Soult's son, the Marquis Oudinot, established the tradition of the carousel in 1825. The famous "Cadre Noir" still perpetuates the "Great School" and the chivalrous traditions, even now.
The officers and "juniors" valiantly defended the Loire in 1940. Inside the castle, a great number of works of art are housed. The decorative arts museum exhibits enamel work, sculptures in wood, trapestries (XVth and XVIth centuries), faience and porcelaine china (XVIIth and XVIIIthe centuries) and period furniture. The horse museum evokes the history of the horse and exhibits collections from all countries.
Once the governor of SAUMUR' dwelling under the reign of LOUIS XIV and LOUIS XV, the castle was transformed into a prison and barracks and then became the property of the town.

76 - Overall view of the castle

77 - The XIVth and XVIth century castle and the Loire

78 - The Horse Museum - A Middle Age antique room

79 - The Decorative Arts Museum
Faience china from Nevers, 2nd half of XVIIth century
Aiguiere with its Chinese decor

80 - The Decorative Arts Museum
XVIIIth century statues - Faience china from Nevers
St. James and St. Stephen

81 - The Horse Museum - The Asian Section - XVIIIth century tapestry - the Royal carrousel

Ussé

A fairyland castle

Ussé, with its white battlemented towers, peppercorn roofs and pinnacled skylights, stands out against a background of meadowland and forest. It could have been designed as a model for an artist wanting to illustrate our finest tales of days gone by. Usse was first and foremost a fortified castle in the depths of the forest. Antoine de Bueil, married to a daughter of Charles VII and Agnes Sorel, started reconstruction work, but in 1485, the estate was sold to the Angevin and Breton Espinay family. Jacques d'Espinay summoned the skills of the architect de l'Epine, to build the charming residence which stands out against the austere nobility of the former fortified walls.
In the XVII century, Usse belonged to Bernin de Vallentinay, cousin of Vaubin. The famous engineer would come and take holidays there after his great construction projects. A room was prepared there for the king who had promised to honour Usse with his presence. This architectural jewel is highly representative of the Renaissance - it leaves an unforgettable impression. The French gardens make this dazzling home all the more pleasant. Today Usse belongs to the Marquis of Blacas.

82 - Ussé - The Castle
83 - The Chapel
84 - XVIth century Italian cabinet
85 - A period toilet service belonging to the Duchess of Duras and a tapestry from Brussels
86 - The King's bedchamber

85

86

88

Villandry

A noble house with famous gardens

All that survives of the strong feudal castle where Philip Augustus and Henry Plantagenet of England met to make peace is the keep, a large square tower dominating the elegant Renaissance building erected in 1532 by Jean le Breton, president of the Blois Exchequer. This senior judge was a man of great taste, fascinated by architecture, who had been chosen by Francis I to monitor the work in his palaces at Fontainebleau and Chambord.
This wonderful castle is also famous for the magical beauty of its gardens laid out by Doctor Carvallo. They follow the plans of the famous landscape gardener Androuet de Cerceau.

87 - Villandry - The renaissance gardens
88 - The flower garden
89 - The box-tree embroideries and the moats
90 - The inner courtyard

89

90

THE LOIRE CASTLES

Baron Armel de Wismes is the author of numerous works, including: "*Ainsi vivaient les Français*" — "Des Croisades à la Troisième République" (Laffont) — "*Jean Bart et la guerre de Course*" (Gallimard) — "*Nantes et le Pays Nantais*" "*Les Chevaliers de Malte*" — "*Ainsi vivaient les marins*" (France Empire) — "Découverte de la Bretagne" (Hier et Demain) — "*La vie quotidienne dans les ports bretons aux XVIIe et XVIIIe siècles*" — "*Histoire de la Vendée*" (Hachette) — "*Corsaires et aventuriers bretons*" (Beauval) — "*Nantes et le temps des négriers*" (France Empire), etc...

On the front cover
Castle of Chenonceau

On the back cover
Castle of Chambord